It's all about…

TOUGH
TRACTORS

KINGFISHER
NEW YORK

KINGFISHER
LONDON & NEW YORK

Copyright © Macmillan Publishers International Ltd 2016
Published in the United States by Kingfisher,
175 Fifth Ave., New York, NY 10010
Kingfisher is an imprint of Macmillan Children's Books, London
All rights reserved.

Distributed in the U.S. and Canada by Macmillan,
175 Fifth Ave., New York, NY 10010

Library of Congress Cataloging-in-Publication data
has been applied for.

Series editor: Sarah Snashall
Series design: Anthony Hannant (LittleRedAnt)
Adapted from an original text by Hannah Wilson

ISBN 978-0-7534-7285-9

Kingfisher books are available for special promotions
and premiums. For details contact: Special Markets
Department, Macmillan, 175 Fifth Ave.,
New York, NY 10010.

For more information, please visit
www.kingfisherbooks.com

Printed in China

9 8 7 6 5 4 3 2 1

1TR/0616/WKT/UG/128MA

Picture credits
The Publisher would like to thank the following for permission to reproduce their material.
Top = t; Bottom = b; Center = c; Left = l; Right = r
Front cover, p1 Shutterstock/smereka; Back cover Shutterstock/Smileus; Pages 2–3, 15b,
30–31 Shutterstock/AFNR; 4 AGCO Corp; 5 Shutterstock/Natalya Prokopenko; 5t Shutterstock/
vevchic; 6 Shutterstock/Jeff Dalton; 7 Getty/Science and Society Picture Library; 8–9 CLAAS
KGaA mbH; 8b Shutterstock/chiqui; 9t Shutterstock/tanger; 10, 11t Shutterstock/BasPhoto;
11b Shutterstock/Pierre-Jean Durieu; 12–13, 17b Shutterstock/smereka; 13t Shutterstock/
Stockr; 14 New Holland Agriculture Ltd; 15t Shutterstock/abdulrazak; 16 Shutterstock/
papa1266; 17t Shutterstock/Kletr; 18–19 Shutterstock/B Franklin; 19t Shutterstock/Dmitry
Kalinovsky; 20–21 Alamy/HotShots; 21t Getty/Ofer Zidron/Stocktrek Images; 22–23 CNH
Industrial America LLC; 22b Nokian Heavy Tyres Ltd/Jarkko Puikkonen; 24 ASIrobots;
25t Pforzheim University/Chrisoph Proessler; 25b Valtra Inc; 26–27 Alamy/Simon Perkin;
26b Getty/National Geographic/Jack Fletcher; 28–29 Alamy/picturesbyrob; 32 Shutterstock/
Photobac.
Cards: Front tl AGCO Corp; tr SAME DEUTZ-FAHR GROUP SpA; bl Tomy36; br CNH Industrial
America LLC; Back tl J C Bamford Excavators Ltd; tr CLAAS KGaA mbH; bl Husqvarna Group;
br Deere & Company.

Front cover: Case IH 7220 tractor pulling a trailer for a combine harvester.

CONTENTS

What is a tractor?   4

The first tractors   6

Big and tough   8

Plowing work   10

Planting and spraying   12

Combine harvesters   14

Other jobs   16

Backhoe loaders   18

Tractors at war   20

Mega tractors   22

Future tractors   24

Dancing tractors   26

Tractor pulls   28

Glossary   30

Index   32

What is a tractor?

A tractor is a very strong vehicle with huge tires. Tractors are not fast but they can drive over the bumpiest, muddiest, or snowiest ground. They can push rocks or pull the heaviest trailers.

In 2014, Manon Ossevoort drove her Massey Ferguson tractor to the South Pole.

FACT ...

The power of a tractor's engine is measured in horsepower (hp); 1 hp is the strength of one horse.

A tractor is the most important vehicle on a farm.

SPOTLIGHT: John Deere 9R series

Famous for:	one of the best-selling tractors
Built by:	John Deere
Built:	2011
Engine power:	up to 670 horsepower

The first tractors

The earliest tractors were steam traction engines that were designed to replace horses. They looked a bit like trains and ran on coal. The first diesel tractors were built in the 1920s.

The first tractors were powered by steam engines.

SPOTLIGHT: Ivel Agricultural Motor

Famous for:	first light farm tractor
Built by:	Daniel Albone
Built:	1901
Engine power:	8 horsepower

The Ivel Agricultural Motor was a very successful early tractor.

Big and tough

Tractors are big strong machines. They have huge wheels to grip the ground. A large diesel engine gives the tractor the power to pull heavy equipment over bumpy surfaces.

Tires have deep treads to grip mud.

The hydraulic hitch raises and lowers attachments.

The power takeoff provides power to the attachments.

The drawbar links to the tractor attachments.

This tractor has an extra set of wheels to give it more grip.

The high cab with glass sides allows the farmer to see clearly.

The powerful diesel engine is good at pulling heavy machines.

The smaller front wheels help steer the tractor.

A weight on the front stops the tractor tipping backward.

9

Plowing work

Farmers who grow crops use different machines that attach to the back of their tractor. To prepare a field for planting, a farmer will use a plow to create a trench of fresh earth called a furrow.

A plow cuts the soil and turns it over to bury the old crops and weeds.

Plowing competitions test who can plow the neatest and straightest furrows.

FACT ...

The first plows were pulled by oxen. Many farmers across the world still use oxen to pull their plows.

Planting and spraying

When the time is right for planting, the farmer attaches a seed drill to the back of the tractor. The seed drill uses tubes and drills to plant and cover seeds evenly across the field.

A sprayer attachment sprays crops with fertilizer or insecticide.

FACT ...

Over 2000 years ago, farmers in ancient Babylon (modern Iraq) used a simple seed drill.

Farmers using a seed drill grow more plants and can have up to eight times more produce to sell.

Combine harvesters

If your field is four miles (seven kilometers) long, you will need a big machine to harvest it—this machine is a combine harvester. A combine cuts down cereal crops and separates the grain from the stalks.

SPOTLIGHT: New Holland CR10.90

Famous for:	most powerful combine harvester
Built by:	New Holland
Built:	2014
Engine power:	652 horsepower

A tractor pulling a trailer collects the grain from the combine harvester.

A hay baler gathers up the stalks.

A fleet of combine harvesters is needed to harvest vast soybean fields in Brazil.

Other jobs

Tractors are not just great at pulling—they are good at lifting and pushing too. This makes them useful for clearing and building. Bulldozers with huge buckets can move rocks and break down walls. Excavators can dig out the hardest rock and concrete.

A bulldozer is a tractor with a large bucket in the front.

A tractor with a strong grapple on its long arm is used to clear trees.

An excavator with a bucket on a long arm is used for digging.

Backhoe loaders

The most useful tractor for the building industry is called a backhoe loader. Its long arm and bucket at the back can reach and dig. Its front bucket can scoop and lift. It can be used in road building, snow clearing, demolition, and mining.

loader

bucket

A backhoe loader is often simply called a digger.

cab

backhoe

stick

boom

rear bucket

stabilizing leg

19

Tractors at war

When countries are at war with each other, tractors can help to build defenses and clear paths. They can also be used to destroy buildings that have become unsafe.

Army tractors are often desert colored.

The JCB HMEE backhoe loader has a lower than normal cab to keep the driver safe.

Mega tractors

One of the strongest production tractors in the world is the Steiger Quadtrac 620. It has enormous crawler wheels to spread its weight over the ground and make it go faster.

The Valtra T234 tractor holds the record for the world's fastest tractor.

FACT...

The largest farm tractor in the world is the Big Bud 747. It is 14 feet (4.25 meters) tall and each of its tires measures 8 feet (2.4 meters) across.

SPOTLIGHT: Steiger Quadtrac 620

Famous for:	one of the strongest tractors
Built by:	Case IH
Built:	2014
Engine power:	683 horsepower

Future tractors

So what next for tractors? Will farmers soon be using robot tractors? Driverless tractors can work alongside a farmer, and even through the night, if they are programed correctly.

Driverless tractors use GPS (Global Positioning System) technology to carry out jobs on a farm.

A Bolid tractor is designed to be operated by a farmer in a helicopter.

FACT ...

The manufacturer John Deere tried to develop a walking tractor that could travel down mountains and through mud. The design was abandoned.

What will farm tractors look like in the future?

Dancing tractors

It takes great skill to drive a tractor over bumpy ground without tipping it backward or onto its side. And it takes great skill to make a tractor dance! But that is what some tractor drivers do to entertain people at agricultural shows.

Square-dancing tractors dance in formation.

FACT ...

The JCB Dancing Diggers pass each other with only inches to spare.

The drivers of the JCB Dancing Diggers perform a "handstand."

Tractor pulls

Which is the most powerful motor sport that uses wheeled vehicles? Motorbike racing? No. Sports car racing? No. Tractor pulling? Yes! At a tractor pulling competition, powerful tractors fitted with extra engines pull a very heavy sled along a 300-foot (100-meter) track.

FACT ...

Adapted tractors at a tractor pulling competition can have an engine strength of 10,000 horsepower. That's the same as the strength of 10,000 horses!

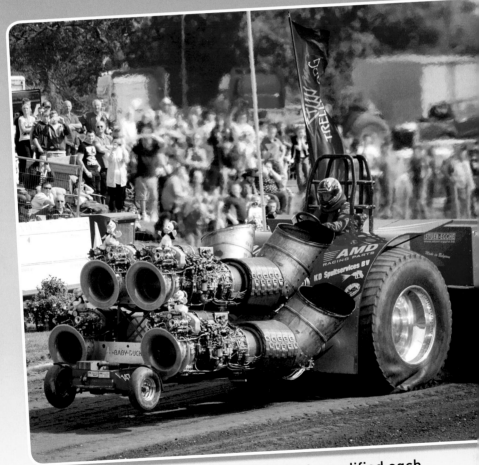

This tractor is called Baby Duck. It is modified each year and has won several European championships.

GLOSSARY

agricultural Anything to do with farming.

attachments Mechanical items that can be hooked onto a tractor.

combustion engine An engine that burns fuel to power a machine.

concrete A building material made of sand, stones, and cement.

crawler wheels Wheels that run inside a metal loop. They have a better grip than normal wheels.

defenses Structures that are built to protect people or buildings.

demolition Knocking something down.

diesel engine An engine that burns diesel fuel to power a machine.

excavator A huge tractor with an enormous bucket for digging and moving earth or rocks.

grain The nutlike part of a cereal crop.

grapples Handlike grips that are attached to a long tractor arm.

hydraulic hitch A lifting mechanism that positions an attachment at the height required by the farmer for the job.

plow A series of discs and blades that break up soil ready for planting.

stabilizing Stopping something from giving way or falling over.

stalk The stem of a plant.

traction engine A road vehicle that is used to pull very heavy loads. Traction engines are powered by either steam or diesel fuel.

trailer A wheeled cart that can be pulled behind a vehicle.

treads The raised parts of a tire.

vehicle A machine that can move and take people or things from place to place. Cars, trucks, buses, and tractors are vehicles.

INDEX

attachments 10, 13

backhoe loaders 18–19, 21

Big Bud 747 23

bulldozers 16

combine harvesters 14–15

Dancing Diggers 26–27

defense tractors 20–21

driverless tractors 24

engines 5, 6, 7, 8, 9, 14, 23, 28, 29

excavators 16, 17

farms 5, 7, 10, 11, 12, 13, 14, 15, 23, 25

fastest tractor 22

fields 10, 12, 14, 15, 22

hay balers 15

Ivel Agricultural Motor 7

JCB HMEE backhoe loader 21

John Deere 5, 25

Massey Ferguson 4

New Holland CR 10.90 14

plow 10–11

plowing competitions 11

seed drills 12, 13

square-dancing tractors 26

steam 6

Steiger Quadtrac 620 22, 23

traction engines 6

tractor pulls 28–29

trailers 4, 14

Valtra T234 22

walking tractor 25